READY, SET, DRAW!

HORSES
YOU CAN DRAW

Nicole Brecke

Patricia M. Stockland

M Millbrook Press / Minneapolis

The images in this book are used with the permission of: iStockphoto.com/Dzianis Miraniuk, p. 4; iStockphoto.com, pp. 4, 5, 22–23; iStockphoto.com/Boris Yankov, p. 5; iStockphoto.com/JR Trice, p. 5; iStockphoto.com/Elena Elisseeva, p. 7; iStockphoto.com/Bram Janssens, 9; iStockphoto.com/Christian Sawicki, p. 11; iStockphoto.com/Corey Sundahl, pp. 14–15; iStockphoto.com/Alexander Hafemann, pp. 18–19; iStockphoto.com/Ingmar Wesemann, p. 26–27; iStockphoto.com/Ricardo De Mattos, pp. 30–31.

Front cover: © iStockphoto.com/Corey Sundahl (barn); © iStockphoto.com/Ingmar Wesemann (field); © Michaela Stejskalova/Shutterstock Images (hand).

Edited by Mari Kesselring
Research by Emily Temple

Text and illustrations copyright © 2010 by Lerner Publishing Group, Inc.

Millbrook Press
A division of Lerner Publishing Group, Inc.
241 First Avenue North
Minneapolis, MN 55401 U.S.A.

Website address: www.lernerbooks.com

Library of Congress Cataloging-in-Publication Data

Brecke, Nicole.
        Horses you can draw / by Nicole Brecke and Patricia M. Stockland ; illustrations by
Nicole Brecke.
            p.   cm. — (Ready, set, draw!)
        Includes index.
        ISBN: 978–0–7613–4160–4 (lib. bdg. : alk. paper)
        1. Horses in art—Juvenile literature. 2. Drawing—Technique—Juvenile literature.
I. Stockland, Patricia M. II. Title.
NC783.8.H65B74 2010
704.9'432—dc22
                                                                    2008052180

Manufactured in the United States of America
2 – BP – 4/1/10

TABLE OF CONTENTS

ABOUT THIS BOOK

Horses are majestic mammals. And they're fun to draw! With the help of this book, you can start sketching your favorites. Draw a high-stepping, graceful Lipizzan. Or color a wild, spirited Mustang. You'll soon know how to draw many types of horses.

Follow these steps to create each horse. Each drawing begins with a basic form. The form is made up of a line and a shape or two. These lines and shapes will help you make your drawing the correct size.

A First, read all the steps and look at the pictures. Then use a pencil to lightly draw the line and shapes shown in RED. You will erase these lines later.

B Next, draw the lines shown in BLUE.

C Keep going! Once you have completed a step, the color of the line changes to BLACK. Follow the BLUE line until you're done.

WHAT YOU WILL NEED

PENCIL SHARPENER

COLORED PENCILS

HELPFUL HINTS

Be creative. Follow your imagination. Read about your favorite horse, and then follow the steps to create your own stable of stallions and mares!

Practice drawing different lines and shapes. All your drawings will start with these.

Use very light pencil lines when you are drawing.

Helpful tips and hints will offer you good ideas on making the most of your sketch.

Colors are exciting. Try to use a variety of shades. This will add value, or depth, to your finished drawings.

Keep practicing, and have fun!

ERASER

PENCIL

PAPER

HOW TO DRAW A CLYDESDALE

Do you love big draft horses (horses used for pulling loads)? Then a Clydesdale might be your favorite breed. These beauties weigh around 2,000 pounds (907 kilograms) and can be 18 hands high. (A hand is about 4 inches, or 10 centimeters.) Clydesdales are calm horses. They are also active and graceful. Clydesdales have heavy feathering, or long hairs, near their hooves. Most are brown or bay (red with a black mane and tail). But some Clydesdales are gray, black, or roan (a dark color flecked with white).

1 Lightly draw an angled baseline and an oval. Add two larger circles. Draw the rump, backbone, and neck.

2 Add a back leg with a big hoof. Draw the belly and a front leg with a big hoof. Add the other two legs and the chest.

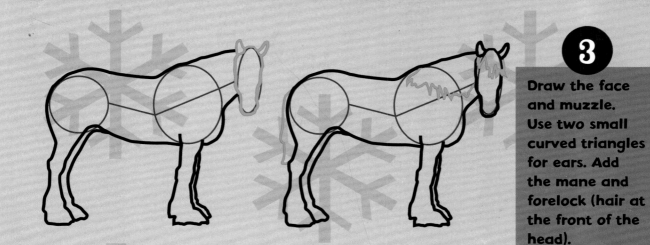

Draw the face and muzzle. Use two small curved triangles for ears. Add the mane and forelock (hair at the front of the head).

4

Erase your baseline and shapes. Draw a small eye and two nostrils.

5 Now it's time to color your Clydesdale!

DRAW A LIPIZZAN

Lipizzans are rare. These intelligent horses were originally bred in Europe for speed and grace. They nearly became extinct, or died out forever. But U.S. troops rescued the Lipizzan at the end of World War II (1939–1945). Today, Lipizzans perform in dressage competitions, which show the art of training and riding. They also pull carriages. Lipizzans perform in shows around the world. These mostly white horses are born brown or black. As adults, they grow to between 15 and 16 hands high.

1 Lightly draw an L-shaped baseline and a small circle. Add an oval. Draw the neck and backbone. Add the ears, muzzle, jaw, and the front of the neck.

2

Make a curved front leg and a small hoof. Draw the stomach line. Add a curved back leg. Add the other front leg and the other back leg. Draw a mane and a long tail.

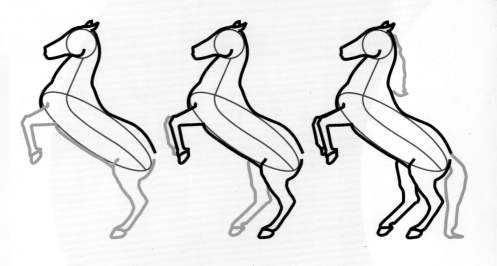

3 Carefully erase your baseline and shapes. Add a small forelock, an eye, and a nostril.

4 Now it's time to color your Lipizzan!

HOW TO DRAW A SHETLAND PONY

Ponies are the smallest types of horse. Shetland ponies are from the Shetland Islands of Scotland. They have possibly existed for ten thousand years! These little powerhouses came to North America around 1885. Shetlands measure only about 10 hands high. This compact breed has short, strong legs and a thick body. Shetland ponies are strong, though. A Shetland can carry half of its own body weight. Shetlands have thick, wavy manes and tails, which help protect them against bad weather.

1 Draw a light, slightly curved baseline and a skinny oval. Add two circles.

2 Connect the two circles with the backbone. Add a back leg and the belly. Make another back leg and two front legs.

3 Draw the top of the mane and the forelock. Add the side of the mane, the tail, and the muzzle.

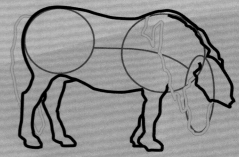

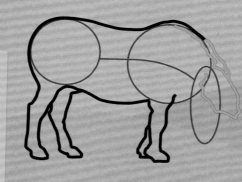

4 Erase your baseline and shapes.

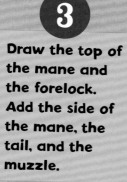

5 Add two triangles for ears. Use a teardrop shape for the eye. Make a small nostril.

6 Now it's time to color your Shetland pony!

HOW TO DRAW AN AMERICAN QUARTER HORSE

The American quarter horse is the first all-American breed. It descended from Spanish and Thoroughbred horses. Early U.S. settlers used to race these horses for quarter-mile (0.4-kilometer) distances. That's how this breed got its name! American quarter horses are able to sprint the quarter-mile distance faster than any other horse. Quarter horses are often used for working with cattle. They stand around 14 to 16 hands high. And they have large hindquarters and powerful forelegs. These qualities make them perfect for ranch work, where they need to turn and sprint quickly. Most quarter horses are chestnut (reddish brown) in color.

1 Drawing lightly, make a slanted base oval and an angled line. Add two larger circles—one at the angle and one at the end of the line.

2 Draw the neckline, backbone, and rump.

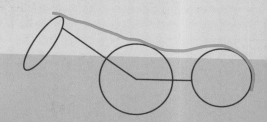

 3

Add pointed ears and the muzzle. Draw the front of the neck and chest.

4

Draw a straight front leg. Add a curved belly and a straight back leg. Draw the other two legs.

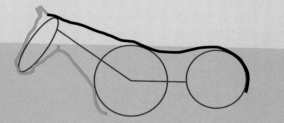

 5 Draw a small forelock and the mane. Add a long, wavy tail.

6 Carefully erase your base shapes and center line.

7 Draw a small eye. Add a line for the nostril and another line for the mouth.

SADDLE UP

American quarter horses wear Western saddles when they're working on the ranch.

DRAW A WESTERN SADDLE!

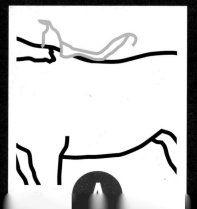

A

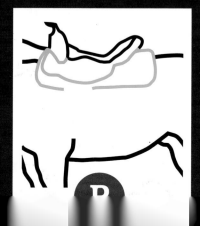

B

C

American quarter horses are popular for trail riding.

8 Now it's time to color your American quarter horse!

HOW TO DRAW AN ARABIAN

The Arabian breed has been around for more than two thousand years! People consider Arabians to be the oldest and purest of all horse breeds. Arabians are known for their gentle personalities. These horses have smaller, sleeker bodies than most breeds. They grow to be 14 to 15 hands high. Arabians have short heads and tapered—or gradually narrowing—muzzles. Their large eyes and nostrils and silky manes and tails make this an attractive breed. Arabians can be bay, black, chestnut, or gray.

1

Draw a longer curved center line and a small base circle. Add two larger circles.

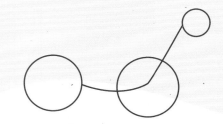

2 Draw two pointy ears. Add a long neckline and backbone.

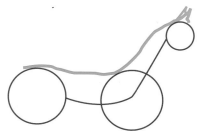

3 Draw the muzzle, the front of the neck, and the chest.

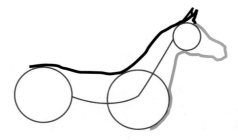

 4 Add a straight front leg and hoof. Add the belly. Then add a stepping back leg, curved hip, and pointing hoof. Draw the other front leg and hoof stepping. Add a standing back leg and hoof.

 5

Add a flowing mane to the back of the neck. Draw a perked-up tail.

6 Carefully erase your center line and base shapes.

7 Add a small eye and a small line for the mouth.

HIGH STEPPING

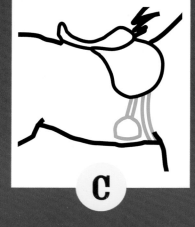

English saddles are used during dressage events. These saddles have clean, light lines.

DRAW AN ENGLISH SADDLE!

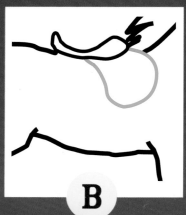

A   **B**   **C**

ARABIANS are from Arabia, an area in southwest Asia that's mostly desert. These horses can handle the heat.

 8 Now it's time to color your Arabian!

TRY THIS
Make the mane, tail, and coat dark to create a black stallion.

HOW TO DRAW A MUSTANG

Mustangs are related to Spanish horses that were brought to North America. Their bodies are equipped for life in the desert or savanna (tropical grasslands). American Indians and white settlers used Mustangs for travel and work. These fast and graceful horses stand between 13 and 15 hands high. Mustangs can be any color. But they often have golden bodies with black manes, tails, and stockings (an area of color between the hoof and knee). Many Mustangs also have a dorsal stripe. This is a dark line that runs down the back from the mane to the tail. In the western United States, groups of Mustangs run wild.

 Draw a large base circle and a curved line. Add a small circle to the end of the line and a large circle to the middle.

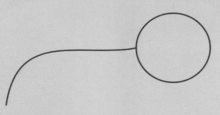

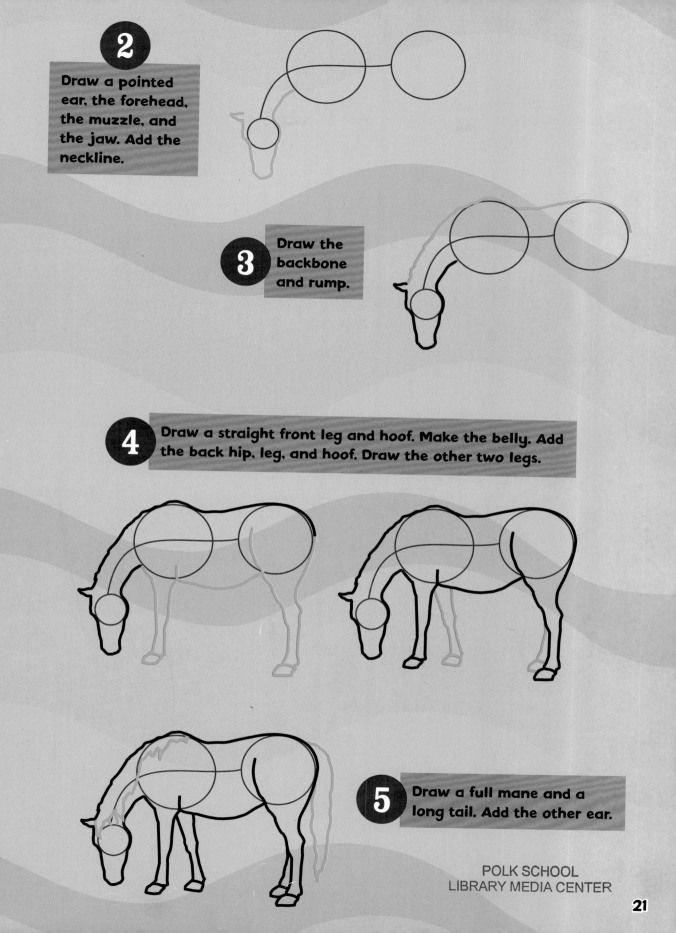

2 Draw a pointed ear, the forehead, the muzzle, and the jaw. Add the neckline.

3 Draw the backbone and rump.

4 Draw a straight front leg and hoof. Make the belly. Add the back hip, leg, and hoof. Draw the other two legs.

5 Draw a full mane and a long tail. Add the other ear.

6 Carefully erase your center line and base shapes before finishing the face.

7 Make a teardrop shape for the eye. Draw a small *U* for the nostril.

Did you know...
SOME PEOPLE
ADOPT
WILD MUSTANGS
AND TRAIN THEM.

8 Now it's time to color your Mustang!

Mustangs have very hard hooves that can hold up on rough ground.

QUICK TIP

Color your lines in the direction the hair grows.

HOW TO DRAW AN APPALOOSA

The Appaloosa is a spotted breed. The Nez Percé Indians of the American Pacific Northwest developed this breed. Appaloosas got their name from the Palouse River, which ran through Nez Percé land. The Appaloosa breed has five different coat patterns: blanket, frost, marble, leopard, and snowflake. Each is a different type of marking and color mix. Appaloosas are used for jumping and racing. They also perform in rodeos and circuses. Appaloosas are known for their energy, strength, and good temperament.

1 Draw a light, angled center line and a small base circle. Add a tilted oval and a larger circle.

2 Draw the backbone, neck, and ears. Add the muzzle and chest.

3 Draw an extended back leg and hoof. Make the belly and an extended front leg and hoof. Add the inside back leg and a stepping front leg.

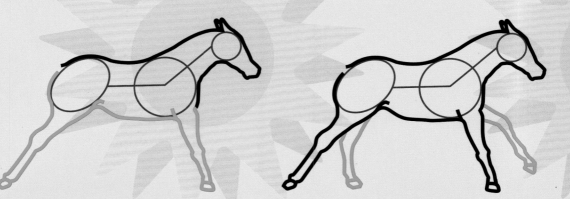

On the neck, add a short mane and forelock. Add a short, flowing tail to the back hip.

Fast Fact...

APPALOOSAS

HAVE SHORT, THIN

TAILS

AND MANES.

5 Erase your center line and base shapes.

6 Draw a small oval for the eye and a circle for the nostril.

HANDY HALTER

Halters help owners handle horses.
Halters also train young horses to wear bridles.

DRAW A HALTER!

A

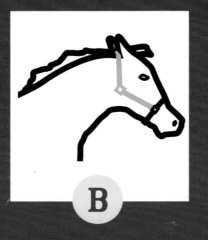

B

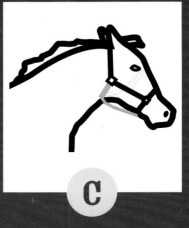

C

EARLY cave paintings in France show images of spotted horses. Some people think these horses may have been related to Appaloosas.

7 Now it's time to color your Appaloosa!

QUICK TIP
Mix colors to add depth.

HOW TO DRAW AN
AMERICAN PAINT HORSE

American paint horses are also known as pintos. They came from Spanish horses. These Spanish horses gave paints their unusual coat patterns. Cowboys began calling this breed paint horses from the Spanish word *pintado*, which means "painted." Paints have two color patterns, ovaro and tobiano. Ovaro is a solid color with large splotches of white. Tobiano is solid white with large splashes of color. These colorful horses stand between 15 and 16 hands high.

1

Draw a light base circle with a line through the middle. Extend that line out to make a center line. Add a large oval around the center line.

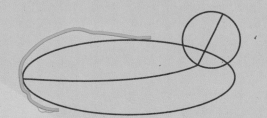

2 Outline the oval for the rump and part of the backbone.

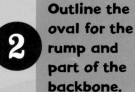

3

Draw a curved back leg and a pointed hoof. Make a short line for the belly. Add one front leg. Use a small, rough circle for the hoof. Add a second front leg.

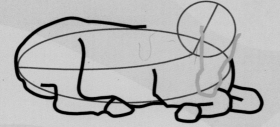

4 Add a muzzle, forehead, and two pointy ears to the right half of the base circle.

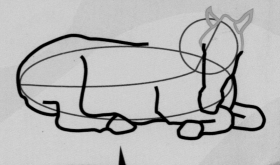

Did you know...

THE TAIL OF A TOBIANO PAINT IS OFTEN TWO DIFFERENT

5 Draw a shaggy forelock, mane, and tail.

6 Carefully erase your base shapes and center line.

7 Draw two small, almond shapes for the eyes. Add two small ovals for nostrils.

EACH American paint has its own unique pattern. The pattern is similar to a fingerprint.

This bright, strong breed is popular for trail riding.

8 Now it's time to color your American paint horse!

QUICK FACT
Horses can sleep standing up!

FURTHER READING

Harrison, Hazel. *The Encyclopedia of Drawing Techniques*. Philadelphia: Running Press, 2004.

Henderson, Carolyn. *Horse & Pony Book*. New York: DK Publishing, 2007.

HorseFun
http://horsefun.com

Horses 4 Kids
http://horses4kids.com

Kids and Horses: Therapeutic Riding Center
http://www.kidsandhorses.org

Ledu, Stephanie. *The Horse Lover's Book*. San Anselmo, CA: Treasure Bay, 2008.

INDEX